Fact Finders®

PEOPLE YOU
SHOULD KNOW

STAN LEE

Get to Know the Comics Creator

by Cristina Oxtra

Consultant: Arie Kaplan
Graphic novelist and author of *From Krakow to Krypton: Jews and Comic Books*

CAPSTONE PRESS
a capstone imprint

Fact Finders Books are published by Capstone Press, an imprint of Capstone.
1710 Roe Crest Drive, North Mankato, Minnesota 56003
www.capstonepub.com

Library of Congress Cataloging-in-Publication Data is available on the Library of Congress website.
ISBN 978-1-5435-9110-1 (library binding)
ISBN 978-1-4966-6582-9 (paperback)
ISBN 978-1-5435-9112-5 (eBook PDF)

Summary: Stan Lee is one of the most influential people in the comic book world. The memorable heroes he created, including Spider-Man, Iron Man, the X-Men, and Daredevil, helped build Marvel Comics into the publishing powerhouse we know today.

Photo Credits
Alamy: Art Directors & TRIP, 20, Creative Stock, 18, 22, Moviestore Collection Ltd., 5, 24, RP Library, 14; AP Images: Invision/Chris Pizzello, cover; Bridgeman Images: Captain America, 12; Getty Images: Bettmann, 17, Corbis/Kim Kulish, 6, Newsday/Gerald S. Williams, 23; Newscom: Glasshouse Images, 8, Zuma Press/Caters News, 10, Zuma Press/Jonathan Alcorn, 27; Shutterstock: RoidRanger, 28

Design Elements by Shutterstock

Editorial Credits
Mari Bolte, editor; Dina Her, designer; Sveltlana Zhurkin, media researcher; Tori Abraham, production specialist

Source Notes
page 7, line 1: Christina Schoellkopf. "'Avengers: Endgame' Marks Stan Lee's Final Cameo: 'It Was Like Santa Came to Set.'" https://www.latimes.com/entertainment/movies/la-et-mn-avengers-endgame-premiere-stan-lee-chris-hemsworth-20190423-story.html. Viewed August 1, 2019.

page 7, line 5: Huw Fullerton. "Stan Lee's Final Movie Cameo Will be a 'Suitable Endpoint' and 'Very Fitting,' Says Avengers: Endgame Directors." https://www.radiotimes.com/news/film/2019-04-24/stan-lees-final-movie-cameo-will-be-a-suitable-endpoint-and-very-fitting-say-avengers-endgame-directors/. Viewed July 12, 2019.

page 9, line 3: Lee, Stan, and George Mair. Excelsior! The Amazing Life of Stan Lee. New York: Fireside, 2002, p. 9.

page 10, line 2: ibid., p. 10.

page 11, line 6: ibid., p. 18–19

page 13, line 1: Lori Dorn. "Stan Lee Opens Up About the Voracious Childhood Reading Habits That Led Him to His Marvel Storytelling." https://laughingsquid.com/stan-lee-marvel-storytelling/. Viewed July 15, 2019.

page 17, line 5: New York Times. "Remembering Stan Lee." https://www.youtube.com/watch?time_continue=143&v=nQGKjlTbIWg. Viewed July 15, 2019.

page 21, line 1: Bethonie Butler. "Stan Lee Used His Platform to Call Out Racism in the 1960s—And He Never Stopped." https://www.washingtonpost.com/arts-entertainment/2018/11/12/stan-lee-used-his-platform-call-out-racism-s-he-never-stopped/?utm_term=.b3ced7d95bd4. Viewed July 21, 2019.

page 22, line 8: ibid.

page 29, line 3: Laughingplace. "Kevin Smith Introduction at Stan Lee Tribute in Hollywood." https://www.youtube.com/watch?v=8Ov_Fbn7yzU. Viewed August 1, 2019.

All internet sites appearing in back matter were available and accurate when this book was sent to press.

Printed in the United States of America.
003183

TABLE OF CONTENTS

1

WITH GREAT POWER

In the movie *Avengers: Endgame,* Tony Stark and Steve Rogers have traveled back in time to 1970. Their goal: to find the Space Stone before the villain, Thanos, can get to it. The pair of heroes walk toward a military base.

Suddenly, a white sports car speeds past. A bumper sticker with comics creator Stan Lee's catchphrase, "'Nuff Said," decorates the car. The camera turns to the driver, who yells, "Make love, not war!" to the soldiers outside the base. The driver was, of course, the one and only Stan Lee.

DID YOU KNOW

Stan's first live cameo was on the TV movie *The Trial of the Incredible Hulk* in 1989. He played a jury member in a trial imagined by the Hulk's **alter ego**, Bruce Banner.

Stan was a familiar face in his Marvel creations. In the 1960s, artists would draw him onto covers or into scenes as a fun gag. But he would also make personal appearances in cartoons, television shows, and movies. His most famous **cameos** were in the first 22 Marvel Cinematic Universe films, starting with *Iron Man* in 2008 and ending with *Avengers: Endgame* in 2019.

Stan made a cameo as a postal worker in the *Fantastic Four* movie that came out in 2005. He joked that the reboot, released in 2015, flopped because he didn't make an appearance.

alter ego—a person's secret personality or different version of themselves
cameo—a brief appearance by a celebrity

Actors, directors, and crew members who had grown up reading Stan's comics were in awe when they met their hero. The days Stan arrived to film his cameos were popular.

Stan loved meeting his fans. He liked that his fans started out young but remained fans throughout their lives.

"People you normally wouldn't even see on the set showed up, and you're like, 'Where did these hundreds of people come from?'" one executive producer remembered.

Endgame director Joe Russo said, "Having Stan on set . . . Look, you have all these movie stars on these movies—and when [Stan] would show up on set, it was like everyone turned into a kid again."

Stan worked hard to gain respect and recognition for comic books and comic book artists and writers. He used his creativity, personal skills, and passion for comics to rise from humble beginnings to superhero stardom. He made Marvel Comics world famous and changed how comic books and superheroes are seen today.

2

ORIGIN STORY

Stanley Martin Lieber was born on December 28, 1922, in New York City. Stan's parents, Celia and Jack, were Romanian Jews. His mother stayed home while his father worked as a fabric cutter in a dress factory. Like millions of Americans, Stan's father lost his job when the Great Depression began in 1929. The family lived in a cramped apartment. Stan's parents slept in the living room, while Stan shared the only bedroom with his younger brother, Larry. His parents often argued about the family's lack of money.

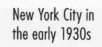
New York City in the early 1930s

Stan escaped the difficulties of his home life through reading.

"In school, reading and composition were always my best subjects. At every meal at home—breakfast, lunch, and dinner—I'd have a book or magazine to read while I ate," said Stan. "My mother used to say that if there was nothing to read, I'd read the labels on ketchup bottles, which I did."

The Great Depression

The Great Depression was the worst economic disaster in the history of the United States. It lasted from 1929 to 1939. The stock market crashed in 1929, wiping out millions of investors. The stock market is where investors buy and sell shares in public companies. With fewer people investing money and fewer products being produced, companies had to lay off workers. By 1933, around 15 million Americans were unemployed.

The first superhero comic was published in 1938. It featured the first appearance of Superman. The comic's success led to more heroes and comics being created.

Stan also wrote his own illustrated stories. "This was a make-believe world I loved because I could retreat to it from the outside—particularly from school," Stan said.

Stan studied hard. His goal was to finish school as soon as possible, so he could get a job to help his family. As the youngest in his class, Stan felt like an outsider. But one teacher, Leon B. Ginsberg Jr., made an impact on him.

"It was Mr. Ginsberg who first made me realize that learning could be fun, that it was easier to reach people, to hold their attention, to get points across, with humor than any other way," Stan said. "It was a lesson I never forgot, a lesson I've tried to apply to everything I do."

DID YOU KNOW?

Stan thought about being a lawyer. He liked the theatrics of a courtroom. But he didn't want to attend law school. After finishing high school, he thought of becoming an actor. He joined a theater group and was in plays. But acting didn't pay much, so he quit. He was also fascinated by advertising.

Stan's part-time jobs as a teenager included writing **obituary** notices for celebrities, delivering sandwiches from a drugstore, and ushering at a movie theater.

Stan graduated from DeWitt Clinton High School in 1939 at age 16. The following year, he applied for a job at Timely Publications, a company that published magazines and comic books. He delivered sandwiches, filled inkwells, and proofed text when needed.

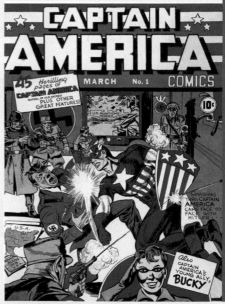

Captain America #1 came out in March 1941. The cover featured Captain America punching Nazi leader Adolf Hitler.

Timely's comics department consisted of editor Joe Simon and artist Jack Kirby. As more comics were created, Joe and Jack needed help. They asked Stan to write. His first work was a two-page text story titled, "The Traitor's Revenge!" It was included in *Captain America #3* in May 1941. Stan's first actual comic book script was in *Captain America #5*. He later wrote stories in other issues and signed them with different names, including S.T. Anley, Stan Martin, and Neel Nats.

obituary—a notice of a person's death

"In those days, grown-ups hated comics, didn't want their children to read them," he remembered. "I figured, I'm not going to use my real name . . . for these silly comic books. So I cut my first name into two, and called myself Stan Lee."

Jack Kirby

Jack Kirby was born in New York City in 1917. He started his career as an animator, drawing *Popeye* cartoons. He worked as a newspaper cartoonist before moving to Timely. There, he and writer-artist Joe Simon created the character Captain America. In the early 1960s, Jack would partner with Stan to create some of Marvel's most well-known characters, including members of the Avengers and the X-Men.

Kirby worked for both Marvel and DC, creating iconic characters and worlds. In 1978, he returned to the animation world as part of Hanna-Barbera's team. He also helped expand the independent comics movement in the 1980s. He retired in 1987 and passed away in 1994.

After a few months, Joe and Jack quit. In 1942, Stan was promoted to editor. By then, the United States had entered World War II (1939–1945). Stan **enlisted** in the U.S. Army. But instead of being sent overseas, he was **designated** as a playwright. He was assigned to the training film division in Queens, New York. He made films and posters to educate troops. In his spare time, he wrote comic book scripts that he sent to Timely.

Stan served in the Signal Corps before being moved to the training film division. Only nine men were given the title playwright.

When the war ended, Stan returned to his editorial job. One day, he met a hat model from England named Joan Clayton Boocock. He and Joan were married in 1947. In 1950, the couple welcomed a daughter, Joan Celia. Three years later, their second daughter, Jan, was born. However, she lived only a few days.

After the war, some comic book publishers began printing scary or gory stories to gain new readers. Other stories included tales of drug use or true-life crime.

In 1954, **psychiatrist** Dr. Fredric Wertham blamed comic books for social problems among teenagers. A Senate committee was formed in Washington, D.C., to investigate. They held a hearing to discuss the "problem of horror and crime comic books." Experts were called to give their opinions. No comic was safe. Even Superman was attacked.

designate—to choose for a particular purpose

enlist—to voluntarily join a branch of the military

psychiatrist—a medical doctor who is trained to treat emotional or mental illness

In response, comics publishers formed the Comics Magazine Association of America. The group established the Comics Code Authority (CCA) to regulate comic books' content. One-third of publishers committed to the Comics Code of 1954. Those who followed the code printed a symbol on the covers of their comic books. Timely, which by this time had changed its name to Atlas, agreed to follow the CCA rules.

The Comics Code of 1954

The Comics Code of 1954 presented a standard that all comics creators were expected to follow. Some rules included:

• not presenting crimes in a way that would make the criminal appear sympathetic, or to make readers mistrust the police or want to commit crimes themselves

• good should always triumph over evil, and the bad guy should always be punished

• banning comics involving zombies, and restricting the use of vampires, ghouls, or werewolves

• using good grammar whenever possible

Comics Code administrator Charles F. Murphy. The image on the left is the original drawing. The image on the right is the same picture after corrections were made so it would fit the Comics Code.

As time went on, Stan grew more frustrated with the public's perception of comic books. Stories were starting to get simple or silly. Even his own publisher was asking for more fight scenes, less story. "There's got to be something better than this," Stan complained later.

Joan told him, "Why don't you write one book the way you'd like to do it?"

The Fantastic Four—the Invisible Woman, Mister Fantastic, the Thing, and the Human Torch—are known as Marvel's First Family.

Superman and Batman had first appeared in Detective Comics in the late 1930s. In 1960, DC brought them back as part of the Justice League—made up of Superman, Batman, Wonder Woman, Aquaman, the Flash, Green Lantern, and Martian Manhunter. They were instantly popular and helped boost the Silver Age of comics.

But Stan wanted to write about characters who were different and surprising. When his publisher asked him for a superhero story, he came up with the Fantastic Four. The Fantastic Four was a team of adventurers who were unlike the perfect heroes that existed at the time. They had fears, doubts, and worries. And although they argued at times, they always put their differences aside to fight the bad guys together.

Published in 1961, *The Fantastic Four* was a revolutionary approach to superhero storytelling. Shortly after, Atlas changed its name to Marvel Comics. The Fantastic Four would help make Marvel one of the top comics companies in the United States.

DID YOU KNOW?

The history of comic books is split into five time periods: The Golden Age (1938–1950), the Silver Age (1950–1970), the Bronze Age (1970–1984), the Copper Age (1985–1993), and the Modern Age (1993–present). However, different experts may disagree on exact dates or the number of ages.

Marvel's success continued with the creation of two new characters. Using the novels *Frankenstein* and *Dr. Jekyll and Mr. Hyde* as inspiration, Stan and Jack Kirby created *The Incredible Hulk*. Tired of seeing teen characters as sidekicks, Stan, with artist Steve Ditko, made a shy, geeky high schooler named Peter Parker the hero in *The Amazing Spider-Man*.

In 1963, Stan and Jack created mutants born with super powers—the *X-Men*. They were heroic but were feared and hated by humans.

In 2018, *The Amazing Spider-Man* became the first Marvel comic to reach its 800th issue.

"Marvel has always been and always will be a reflection of the world right outside our window," Stan said later. "These stories have room for everyone, regardless of their race, gender, or color of their skin. The only things we don't have room for are hatred, intolerance, and bigotry."

Thanks to the new superheroes, Marvel sold 16.1 million comics in 1960. By 1965, they had doubled that amount.

DID YOU KNOW?

The Hulk was originally gray. Stan wanted a color that did not suggest any particular ethnic group. However, the **inking** process at the time did not make the gray consistent on comic book pages. It was easier to color the Hulk green.

inking—the process in making comics that involves outlining the artwork and adding depth and shading

Stan didn't see the inclusion of Black Panther as a big deal. He thought comics should represent everyone in America.

In 1966, Stan and Jack created *Black Panther*, the first black superhero in **mainstream** comics. Featuring T'Challa, the powerful prince of a highly advanced and rich African nation, *Black Panther* broke **stereotypes** and was groundbreaking for its time.

In a Stan's Soapbox column in 1968, Stan wrote, "**Bigotry** and racism are among the deadliest social ills plaguing the world today. It's totally irrational, patently insane to condemn an entire race, to despise an entire nation, to vilify an entire religion. Sooner or later, we must learn to judge each other on our own merits."

DID YOU KNOW?

Stan originally used "Excelsior!" as a way to sign off from his columns. The word, which is also New York's state motto, is Latin for "Ever Upward." Stan's rivals were starting to copy his work, and he wanted a word that would be difficult to spell or explain. He later used it as a motto to inspire people to reach for greatness.

Stan's Soapbox

Stan gave nicknames to Marvel's writers and artists. He called the team "The Bullpen" to create a fun, clubhouse-like atmosphere. Readers could write to Stan and ask him questions. He answered them on a page in every comic book called "Bullpen Bulletins."

He also had a column called "Stan's Soapbox." His most famous phrases, "'Nuff Said" and "Excelsior!", appeared there. For a $1 membership fee, Marvel fans could join a fan club called the "Merry Marvel Marching Society."

Between 1965 and 2001, Stan used "Stan's Soapbox" to write to his readers.

bigotry—treating a person of a different religious, racial, or ethnic group with hatred or intolerance

mainstream—part of the current dominant trend or activity

stereotype—an overly simple opinion of a person, group, or thing

TRUE BELIEVERS UNITE

With his humor, outgoing personality, and vision of what comic books and superheroes could be, Stan became Marvel's spokesman. He spoke at colleges and answered media questions. In 1972, Stan was promoted to publisher and editorial director at Marvel.

In this new role, Stan focused on bringing Marvel's heroes to television and movies. The first to make the jump was *The Incredible Hulk*, which premiered on TV in 1977. Captain America, Spider-Man, and Dr. Strange made their made-for-TV-movie **debuts** soon after. In 1986, Howard the Duck appeared on the big screen.

Blade actor Westley Snipes remembered Stan for his ability to inspire people to be creative.

In the mid-1990s, Marvel formed a department devoted to making movies. *Blade* was Marvel Studios's first movie, released in 1998. The movie was a huge success and paved the way for additional Marvel films.

The first *X-Men* movie was released in 2000. Stan made his first cameo in a movie. He played the role of a hot dog salesman. The 12th movie in the *X-Men* series, *Dark Phoenix*, was released in 2019.

You're My Only Hope

With television's rise in popularity, comic book sales started declining in the 1970s. Marvel might have gone bankrupt except for one project—a series of comics based on a space trilogy. *Star Wars #1* sold more than a million copies. Between 1977 and 1986, 107 issues and three special issues of *Star Wars* were published.

debut—a first appearance

In the 1990s, Stan stepped down as Marvel's publisher. He continued to serve as **executive producer** of many movies featuring Marvel characters. He also continued appearing in cameos. He was spotted in popular movies and shows such as *The Simpsons, The Big Bang Theory, Teen Titans Go! To the Movies,* and *Big Hero 6.*

In 2001, DC Comics asked for new stories. Stan's *Just Imagine* series reinvented popular DC superheroes. He started a YouTube channel, where he answered questions and gave interviews. He narrated Spider-Man and Avengers games and hosted a TV show called *Superhumans.* And he was always a popular guest at comic book conventions.

Stan earned many awards, including a place in the Will Eisner Award Hall of Fame, the Visual Effects Society's Lifetime Achievement Award, and the National Medal of Arts. He also received a star on the Hollywood Walk of Fame.

executive producer—someone who helps get movies made

Even into his 90s, Stan did not slow down. He pushed for more diversity at Marvel. In 2011, Stan worked alongside storyteller Sharad Devarajan to create a teen superhero from Mumbai, India. *Chakra, The Invincible* featured an Indian teen superhero named Raju. In 2013 he created a Chinese hero called *The Annihilator*. His last creation, Jewel, was based on a Chinese pop star.

In 2010, the Stan Lee Foundation, a nonprofit organization, was established. It provides access to literacy, education, and the arts.

On July 6, 2017, Stan's wife, Joan, died of stroke-related complications. A little more than a year later, heart and respiratory failure took Stan's life. On November 12, 2018, comic book fans around the world mourned.

Hundreds of fans visited Stan's star on Hollywood Boulevard after his death. Some wore costumes or left mementos.

Filmmaker, actor, and comic book writer Kevin Smith spoke at a tribute to Stan in Hollywood. "Stan was a man who told simple stories about the worst thing in the world happening, and everybody running away from it. Wisely. Sensibly," Smith said. "But in the midst of that, there's always a handful of people just very colorfully heading right into it. Heading toward danger. Those are the stories the man told. He helped us all build our morality . . . He taught us right from wrong—while entertaining us."

Superheroes never really die because they reside in the memories of their fans. Stan lives on in the hearts of millions of comic book readers. He is alive in the imagination of the creative minds he influenced. His voice is heard in those who truly believe that one person can make a difference.

DID YOU KNOW?

In July 2019, the New York City Council renamed a street in the Bronx Stan Lee Way.

GLOSSARY

alter ego (AHL-tuhr EE-GO)—a person's secret personality or different version of themself

bigotry (BIH-guh-tree)—treating a person of a different religious, racial, or ethnic group with hatred or intolerance

cameo (KA-me-yoh)—a brief appearance by a celebrity

debut (day-BYOO)—a first appearance

designate (DEH-zig-nayt)—to choose for a particular purpose

enlist (in-LIST)—to voluntarily join a branch of the military

executive producer (ig-ZE-kyuh-tiv pruh-DUH-suhr)—someone who helps get movies made; executive producers help pay for the film but do not work on-set

inking (IN-king)—the process in making comics that involves outlining the artwork and adding depth and shading

mainstream (MAYN-streem)—part of the current dominant trend or activity

obituary (oh-BIT-shu-ehr-ee)—a notice of a person's death, usually with a short biographical account

psychiatrist (sye-KYE-uh-trist)—a medical doctor who is trained to treat emotional or mental illness

stereotype (STER-ee-oh-tipe)—an overly simple opinion of a person, group, or thing

READ MORE

Arbona, Alejandro. *Comic Book Creators*. Baltimore, MD: Duo Press, 2019.

Bray, Adam, Lorraine Cink, John Sazaklis, and Sven Wilson. *Marvel: Absolutely Everything You Need To Know.* New York: DK Publishing, 2016.

Learn to Draw Marvel Avengers, Mightiest Heroes Edition. Mission Viejo, CA: Walter Foster Jr., an imprint of The Quarto Group, 2020.

INTERNET SITES

Britannica for Kids. Stan Lee
https://kids.britannica.com/students/article/Stan-Lee/631211

Marvel HQ
https://www.marvelhq.com/comics

Marvel Universe for Young Readers
https://www.marvel.com/comics/discover/140/marvel-universe-for-young-readers

CRITICAL THINKING QUESTIONS

1. Stan used comics to address social issues such as bigotry, racism, and stereotypes. Which of his characters do you most identify with? Why?

2. Readers could write to DC Comics and have their questions answered by Stan. What question, or questions, would you ask?

3. The history of comic books is split into five main time periods (see page 19). Can you find examples of comics from each of those periods? Compare the art and writing styles. How do comics from across periods compare? How are they similar? How are they different?

INDEX